# Some Days are Better Than Others

By Richard Leis

# CONTENTS

Introduction     3

Chapter 1.    Some Days are Better Than Others     4

Chapter 2.    911 Emergency     10

Chapter 3.    A View Through Our Window     17

Chapter 4.    Pack Rats     25

Chapter 5.    A Boy and His Dog     32

Chapter 6.    The Camping Trip from Hell     43

Chapter 7.    Dead or Alive it's off to School     48

Chapter 8.    Men are Definitely not Women     52

Chapter 9.    "When He Loves Me does He really…?     56

# Introduction

Several years ago while preparing to adopt our first of three children from China, I heard about a retired missionary who had lost both legs to advanced diabetes and was very depressed. I got to know his daughter who was also on the waiting list for a child from China. When she mentioned his plight, I decided to write some humorous stories to lift his spirits. I am glad to say that the stories helped to lift his spirits and became quite popular in the facility where he was recovering.

Each of the stories actually happened. In most cases, I have embellished the truth to make the stories more entertaining.


Richard Leis

# Chapter 1

# Some Days are Better Than Others

Marilyn and I should live on a farm. We live in the high desert and take great pleasure feeding living things that come in from miles away. Some we encourage to stay and others we would rather have move on. We even have an "invisible snake" that has taken up residence somewhere in the front atrium area. I call him "invisible" because he only comes out for Marilyn who generally responds by running madly down the street flapping her arms and legs like an earthbound goony bird straining for flight. Steve, our son, and I accused her of making it all up. This all changed one morning when Beauford saw fit to leave his skin on our front porch doormat.

Our outdoor menagerie is rounded out by our two retrievers, and a poodle that has delusions of grandeur. Satchmo and Lady are the retrievers and Giappetto... The three spend their lives bringing things home (another story) or swimming in our pool.

The interior of the house, though, is owned by our cats. I can never remember whether we have seven or eight of them. Periodically, our in-laws drop off their animals during their vacation time. "You'll never notice them." "After all, you have so many!" They all just kind of arrived singly or in multiples, but usually when Marilyn said something like, "Can we have baby?"

We have a large rambling home, so, even though they are indoor cats, we only see a few at any one time. Except, that is, when I start on any project. I think that they get together to plan how to get back at me for their last bath.

Our bathroom sink has a wonderful, cast bronze fixture and drain spout to match. The only problem with it is that the plunger lever would not open or close the stopper. I had an extra few moments and decided that I would get a new drain piece and replace the thirty year old drain pipes at the same time. I wanted to surprise Marilyn. After all, she had only been commenting on the inoperable drain plug for a year or two. She wasn't due home for several hours, plenty of time. Our guests were not due until the evening, about thirty minutes after Marilyn's arrival.

Rule number one: Never get on your back under a sink without being able to see what your cats are up to.

If there was only one cat, there probably wouldn't be a problem, but all eight were gathered around the bathroom like a bunch of vultures waiting for dinner.

I had just begun to tighten the copper, cold water supply pipe when "Runt," our hyperactive, inquisitive Siamese, took a chomp out of my kneecap. Being the calm, coolly collected person that I am, I yelled and yanked the wrench, cleanly breaking the aging copper pipe off at the wall. In my frantic efforts to escape the sudden calamity of ice-cold spray, I scared the vulturous, feline menagerie, sending them flying into every direction. The once pristine, organized bathroom was instantly transformed into the visage of a flooding junkyard. Fur, bottles, and bathroom stuff flew and floated in every direction. Since I had closed the bathroom door, the panic perpetuated itself into a frantic, pulsating demon that would rival any tornado. By this time, our master bathroom was transformed into a riotous pond. I thought, "It is two hours before Marilyn gets home."

It seemed like hours had passed before I could get the door opened. I had inadvertently locked it. The frantic, clawing, growling, panicked furry visage from hell made it almost impossible to get to the door, much less unlocked and opened. A wave of water followed me out of the bathroom, across the Mexican tiled floors and down the hallway ahead of me.

As the cats and I raced down the tiled hallway trying our best to get out of the water, Klondike, our twenty-two pound Manx raced between my legs. I fell headlong, sliding down the hallway as if on some gigantic water slide. Klondike lighted on my back, firmly setting his claws so as not to fall off of his newly acquired surfboard. Eventually, I raced out the back of the house to the water supply cutoff valve. It only took thirty minutes to mop up the mess. I thought, "Only one hour and thirty minutes before Marilyn gets home."

Rule number two: do not forget rule number one.

Within a few moments I had re-soldered the cold water supply and began working on removing the bronze drain and the thirty-year-old pipes. The bathroom vanity is quite large, about five feet long and three feet deep. Before long, all eight cats were inside the sink vanity with me watching my every move with great interest. Usually, each cat has an assigned task. When I am writing, D.C. and Runt watch over my work. Rarely do all eight gather to help. Not this time!

I tend to be single-minded and everything else around me disappears. Everything seemed to be going well. I had removed the old pipes and removed the cast bronze drain and was preparing to put in the new one. I had not noticed that Runt was no longer in the cabinet with me. Runt had exited the vanity and was now positioned inside the sink waiting for the right moment. All of a sudden, this long black thing (his paw) comes dangling out of the hole in the bottom of the sink where the drain had been and nails me right between the eyes. My only thoughts were of Beauford the invisible snake, thinking that he had somehow gotten inside the house. I started, crashing my head against the bottom of the sink causing it to break free off its fasteners. Of course, it fell straight down, breaking the hot water supply pipe and knocking me silly as it landed squarely on the side of my head. All seven cats, trapped inside the cabinet, raced across my chest and out the open bathroom door.

I neglected to say that as I took apart the old pipes, thick, black gooey stuff splattered me and all eight of my buddies. They didn't seem to mind being covered from head to toe. Jazzman, a pure black Manx with a tail, had been rolling in it!

Since I had already done this once, I had gotten vastly quicker at cleanup and repairing my repair work. I now had less than fifteen minutes. I quickly put the bathroom back together, took a quick shower, dressed for our guests and collapsed in a heap on the family room couch just as Marilyn walked in the door. She said, "How did your day go?" "Fine" I said. "It looks like you washed the floors," she said. Not wanting to fess up, I said, "The cats and I fixed the sink stopper." After a brief inspection, Marilyn gave me a thank you kiss and began putting the food out for our guests.

A few moments later I heard her ask, "What is that smell, and why are the cats all gooey and black?" "What is that smell?" I thought, "Where is my cat washing suit?" "I have one half hour before our guests arrive . . ." Some days are just better than others! Some days are just better than others!

# Chapter 2

# 911 Emergency

Before I was married, cats never played a part in my life, unless it was in a zoo. Those cats, of course, were a bit larger. I think that all must think the same thing regardless of size. Several years ago, some friends gave us some wonderful terrazzo floor tile. Each tile weighed about four pounds. Since our family room and kitchen area see a lot of traffic from the swimming pool, we thought that it would be a good opportunity to remedy the cleanup problem. Carpet just likes to grab hold of all kinds of interesting things that animals and playful children leave behind. I have a theory that socks that appear to have been consumed by the black hole in the washer were really hidden away for some unknown purpose by little people in the carpet.

Nine cats and I set to work stripping the old carpet, pad and old linoleum floor tiles. Ivan, a Balinese, was the most helpful. He stood his ground in the middle of the project and looked as if he was directing. Periodically, he would hitch a ride on an old piece of carpet as we drug it through the house. Eventually, we couldn't accommodate Ivan when we began using large, sharp, tile scrapers. Wherever we wanted to go, Ivan stood. There had to be a solution.

I was the only one in the family that did not yet play a musical instrument.

Even the cats show musical ability. The best way to occupy Ivan is to put him in a cylinder cat tree, directly in front of the music system, and turn on classical music. Ivan doesn't just listen--he enjoys the music. In fact, he becomes one with it. He lays his head down facing the speakers; pulls his ears and whiskers back as if in a musical wind, and keeps time with his tail. While watching him, you can almost see the notes racing out of the speakers and rustling his fur. He is not a rock 'n roll cat; he is purely classical. Ivan prefers Brahms and Beethoven over Liszt and Stravinsky. Runt likes Stravinsky. Klondike, our twenty-two pound cat, enjoys everything especially if it is played on our baby grand. Runt prefers the Yamaha upright and is into all the latest stuff. However, he likes the feel of almost any music when played on his piano.

Anyway, we stationed Ivan in his tree in front of the sound system and played Beethoven's Unfinished Symphony.

With Ivan out of the way, we only had eight to deal with. For the most part, the project went smoothly until it came time to spread thin-set on the floor and tiles. Cats have cement and paint magnets. As soon as we would lay down an area of cement-type mastic, the cats would troop through it. For a few seconds they seemed to love the gooey feeling of the grey stuff coming up through their toes. Then they would shake their feet, flinging the goo all over us and anything else that stood in the way. I kept thinking to myself, "Boy, this is fun." It was kind of fun until Shadrak our king size, bigger than life, into everything male Siamese, just lay down in the middle of the tub of thin set. Now, in the middle of everything, I had to dawn my cat-washing suit and give Shadrak a bath. When I was done, the thought occurred to me, "I wonder what he is going to do to get back at me?" Siamese don't get back, they get even.

Anyway, several days later, Marilyn, Steve the cats and I finished the floor. It looked beautiful. We had moved the couch into the family room, but the rest of the furniture was still stacked in our bedroom and living room. Marilyn, Steve, all eight furry friends and I were crashed on the couch watching a video. Shadrak was off doing his own thing, but that was usual for him anyway. He either is pestering the tar out of you for attention or he is in trouble.

It was about eight in the evening and the house was a big mess. We were praying that no one would drop by. All of us looked like we had walked through a batch of cement. Actually, we looked like we had been living in some back ally for about a week. I had just about relaxed when the front door chimes did their thing. The cats were so tired that none of them even raised their heads. My thought was, "All the cars are in the garage, and maybe they will think we aren't here. The chimes rang again, then a third time. I finally got up and went to the door.

The front of our house has an atrium area that is separated from the rest of the world by several walls and a variety of tropical plants. When I opened the door, the automatic porch light was on, but no one was there. Then I heard a voice say from behind the wall, "Step out onto the porch." I thought to myself, "I am not stepping out onto the porch for any unseen person." I started to close the door, when the voice said, "I am a sheriff. Step out onto the porch!" I wasn't real impressed until I noticed that there was a pistol peeking around the wall. It was pointed at me. Once again the voice said, "I said, step out of the house onto the porch." Well, since he said it quite that way, I stepped out. Then I said, "Good evening, officer. What can I do for you?" He said, "Is there anyone else in there with you?" I said, "Yes, my wife and son." I didn't think he would be real impressed if I said, "And my nine cats!" Funny, this deputy must have thought I didn't hear, because he said, "Who is in the house with you?" I then replied, "Marilyn, my wife, my son Steve and our nine cats. That, I think, struck him as kind of odd because he didn't know what to say. By this time, he had slid around the wall and could be seen in full view. He then said, "Close the door all the way." I had--except for a slight crack. I didn't want the cats to come out and I wanted some way to get in if he wasn't who he said he was.

The officer said, "Is there anyone else in there with you that I don't see?" As if to say, "Is there anyone behind the door?"

This kind of circular questioning went on for a while and finally I asked, "What is going on here? Why are you asking these questions?" "Why is your pistol out?" He said, "Do you have any young children in your house?" "No," I replied, "We are all adults." He said, "Don't you know that it is against the law to dial 911 and then hang up?" I said, "Why would anyone want to do that?" "I don't know, but this is really serious." "Someone in your home dialed 911 thirteen times and then just hung up." "Officer, I assure you, no one in our home would ever do anything like that." "Well, I don't believe you" he replied.

I could just see the headlines, "LOCAL PASTOR DIALS 911 THIRTEEN TIMES AS PRACTICAL JOKE."

"Come in, I offered, "and let's ask if anyone else has done this (dastardly deed)." It took a few moments of coaching--he obviously believed that someone dangerous was inside. Finally, he entered. I asked, "Marilyn and Steve, have you been dialing 911 and then hanging up as a practical joke?" Just the look on their faces was enough to let him know that they were not guilty, so his gaze turned back to me. I then began counting my cats. Oh no, Shadrak was missing. I thought, "How do I explain this one?" Sometimes the truth is hard to deal with. Each of our cats is really good at something. Shadrak loved to play the phone. That was his instrument of choice. His favorite phone was the one in our bedroom. It was not only push button, but it had a variety of automatic buttons.

I looked at the policeman. He gave me a look that said, "You are dead meat, buddy. Get your coat." I responded, "Officer, I know how this happened." He said, "I want to hear this." With that, my heart hit my feet. I thought, "He really isn't going to believe this one." Actually, it was more like, "When he hears this one, he is going to handcuff me, and put me directly in jail." "Officer, my cat Shadrak must have dialed the phone." He looked at me like I was some kind of apparition that just exploded from the inside of a Halloween jack-o-lantern. After he worked his way through his emotions, he said, "I don't believe that I heard you correctly." I thought, "I am dead! Wait till this one hits the papers, 'LOCAL PASTOR BLAMES 911 PRANK ON CAT.'"

I said, "Officer, I have a special phone in the bedroom and Shadrak likes to walk on the buttons. He probably dialed 911 just to hear someone talk!" The officer responded, "I could believe that if it only happened one time, but not thirteen times in a row!" "Officer, before this goes any further let's just take a look." We walked back to the master bedroom and there was Shadrak with his foot on one of the phone buttons. Just as we walked in, he stepped down. We could hear the phone dialing, and a voice saying, "911 Emergency Services. How may I help you?"

Much to my relief, the officer started laughing. "I would never have believed it," he said, "if I hadn't seen it." He then picked up the receiver and explained the situation to his fellow officers. Peals of laughter could be heard over the phone.

I thought to myself, "Some days are just better than others."

Chapter 3

# A View Through Our Window

Marilyn, Steve, Lynnae, Kristin and I used to live in Santa Barbara, California. We bought a home that had been owned by a true landscape architect. The house was set back on the property with grand brick walkways and a beautiful tree-lined driveway with a gentle rising slope. Our home was about fifty years old. Aged hardwood floors, and a grand fireplace with the entire mystique only found in an older home fulfilled our pleasure. We also had a guesthouse and a splendid rear yard that was artfully separated into four different flora zones.

Directly behind the guesthouse was a most fascinating and abundant vegetable garden area. It was far beyond most people's imagination or creative ability. Four different compositions of gravel and soil levels all topped a unique drainage system that made it impossible to over water. All of this was kept in place by striations of railroad ties that raised the topsoil four feet above an asphalt bed. Any good plant grew magnificently there. It was a favorite playground of domestic and non-domestic animals.

Directly to the rear of the house was a beautifully sculptured red brick patio with curving serpentine walls backed by towering stands of bamboo. The entire lawn was lined with mortared red brick walkways that all led to a large variety of fruit trees and huge-leafed tropical plants. This was the play area of our three children.

Marilyn and I have very different concepts when it comes to terms like, "I am going shopping. Watch the children for me." My usual response was "Sure." I would put all three kids into this adventure park of a back yard with our Airedale and Chow. After all, since we owned a toy store, there was almost one of every conceivable outdoor toy there to play with. Some were powered by imagination, others, like the merry go round, by water. Much to Marilyn's amazement, our children somehow always survived.

There were few down sides to that tropical paradise, but one was the fruit rats. Unlike city dwellers, they didn't crave meat; they just liked to sample the large variety of fruit in our yard. I was unaware of this unique problem until my daughters came running in from the backyard informing me how these strange looking kitties had scaled the outside of their bedroom wall and disappeared through a hole in the overhang into the attic.

Halloween was always a fun time at our house and business. A Hollywood makeup artist somehow thought that I had rescued him, reorienting his life. As a thank you, he would just appear and want to make one of us up like a "Planet of the Apes" figure, complete with movie costume. On other occasions he would try to transform us into some image of a slithering other world creature or Darth Vader complete with laser sword. During Christmas, he took great pleasure in transforming my 165-pound frame into a large, "marshmellowy" middle old Santa. He would "metamorph" into a six-foot five inch elf. The two of us would set off in our Dodge "Maxi-van" delivering free toys from our store to less fortunate families and children.

It was on Halloween, though, that Barry always made me the object of his special attention. Usually, it was something with lots of hair and long fangs complete with drooling, slimy this and that. It wasn't a matter of just sliding into a rubber mask, but this took hours of careful preparation and application of devices that he had created just for the occasion. The goal was to trick the trickers and playfully treat the treaters.

At that time, we only had four cats and two dogs. I gave the Airedale an Indian name in honor of the area where we purchased him. He was "Washoe." Marilyn named the chow "Chou Su." I am not sure how she came up with the name, but it sounded pretty good until some of our Chinese friends dropped by and started laughing when they heard Marilyn beckon her dog. I asked, "What is so funny?" They replied, "Why did you give your dog the Chinese name for 'hamburger?'" Twenty-two years later, this would influence the nickname of our Chinese daughter, Lexi.

In those days, we had very unique cats. My shadow was a big-hearted black and white male that I called "Rocky." When I was home, that cat had to be with me. I think that he actually knew that I had rescued him on one of my discovery trips to the animal shelter. At night he would not rest until I let him into our bedroom, and he would sleep in the easy chair next to my head as if guarding me while I slept.

The picture was rounded out with a grey tabby, an outspoken Siamese and an all-brown Balinese named "Shawndee." I have always felt that God put that cat into my life to test me! He was trouble from the day we introduced him into our home. He loved to ride in cars and if you wouldn't let him in them, he would jump on top of the car and yell until he found success. One rainy night, Marilyn and the girls were off to the grocery store and Shawndee attempted to get into the car. Marilyn picked him up and put him in the house. Not seeing this whole act of futility, I walked over to the door to wave goodbye. Since it was dark, I didn't see Shawndee jump onto the roof of my wife's Volvo. A few minutes later an amused Marilyn and a very angry, soaked cat returned. When Marilyn had applied the brakes at the corner neighborhood stop sign, Shawndee could not maintain his grip and went surfing down the windshield and hood with all legs and claws extended. When Marilyn opened the car door he jumped in complaining all the way home.

Not only did this cat ride in cars, he loved water and had a unique knack for naturally creating general mayhem. Shawndee had a specialty for mayhem. It was opening doors, not sliding glass doors; a dog could do that, but regular doors with doorknobs. We always had to make sure that the doors were locked to the places where children and Shawndee didn't belong, because he would gain entry quicker than any professional second story man.

In front of our house was a huge elm tree that must have been planted before the house was built. Its canopy draped over the house and provided a sanctuary for climbing children, squirrels, birds, Rocky and Shawndee. When visitors arrived, they had to ascend brick steps, a curving walkway and then climb nine large steps onto an elevated southern style front porch. Shrubs and trees provided a picturesque walkway during the day and a land of terror for human creatures of the night on Halloween. We took advantage of this by mounting speakers and strobe lights in the tree over the porch. The night would begin when I was thoroughly covered with hair, paws, claws, and fangs. The sound effects were prepared, light panel ready to go, lubricant removed from the door hinges so the door would scream out a warning when opened.  The trap was set for any unwary trickster that dare knock and call out "Trick or treat!"  My suit would fool any grown-up. No one could possibly know who I was.  That is, unless they were two, and related.  My son, Steve, waddled over, grabbed my fur and said, "Daddy!"

The interior lights were off.  All was set.  Just a very weak light guided the paths of the unwary. At the knock, the special effects wind and lightning chased madly through the trees, descending upon the special little guests.  Nervous laughter began, some were ready to run.  At the cry "Trick or treat," I began to open the door slowly. My image reflected in their ever-amazed eye balls.  Then with a mighty roar, I yelled "Trick, what have you brought me to eat?"

The parents had all been warned ahead of time.  We all had a great laugh together.  After a few hours, the numbers slowed down to a few repeaters who wanted to discover if it was just as scary the second time.

At the end of a great time, Kristin, Lynnae, Steve, Marilyn, Barry (artist) and I were all sitting on the floor drinking hot cocoa and laughing over the evening's adventure when a thumping started on the front door.  The thumping got louder and louder.  Every few seconds a blood curdling scream would break forth.

Still in my makeup, I headed for the front door with family and friend in close pursuit. "Could there truly be some kind of Halloween apparition that we have annoyed with our antics?" I thought.

When we reached the front door, it began to swing open, the dry hinges screaming with every increasing inch. Shawndee pranced into the living room with a gigantic, live fruit rat in his mouth.

Marilyn and the girls let out blood-curdling screams that most assuredly shattered every window from Santa Barbara to Mexico City. The screams scared the cat that dropped the rat. The rat took off for parts unknown within our home with cats, dogs and a furry, clawed, fanged father in fast pursuit. Our once pleasant lived-in home turned into an image of a rummage sale. When the rat would head under a coach or piece of furniture, all would follow, turning top to turvy. Marilyn would take another series of deep breaths and scream some more. Lights came on all over the neighborhood. I could hear footsteps racing up our walkway. I thought, "How will I ever explain this?"

Finally, I got the glass sliding door to the rear of the house opened, and the rat, cats, dogs and others all followed, roaring and yipping into the night.

A neighbor who was a police lieutenant didn't bother knocking, but rushed in. He said, "Are you all right? What was that screaming? It sounded like someone was being murdered." Soon the wrecked living room filled with friends, all asking the same question. I knew that no one would believe the story about a cat that could open doors. Meanwhile, some of the ladies helped a winded Marilyn down from atop the toilet. All eyes were suspiciously upon me and I finally replied, "Oh, we're just practicing for next Halloween!" We all laughed together, and our guests and friends once again returned to their homes.

It was a night that not only would introduce the antics of Shawndee, but one that we will never forget. After all, the joke was on us. It was a night that we will always remember.

# Chapter 4

# Pack Rats

When my cats and I set out to do home repairs, it seems that it turns into a cataclysmic adventure. We live in Tucson, Arizona and you just never know who will show up to take up permanent residence. Besides our two retrievers and a blind, deaf, toothless poodle we have our curious assortment of pedigree and not so pedigree cats. This is the normal contingent of the adopted Leis household, but there are a variety of animals that seem to adopt us.

Originally, when we moved to Tucson, we lived out in the desert. Those of you from other places probably would call it the country. We could walk out our front door, look into almost any direction, and not be part of a community of houses, schools, apartments and businesses. Now, sadly, that is not so. We live right in the middle of a doctor, lawyer, and professional housing area. Every time new homes would be built, the animals that lived in that space would move to the next empty acreage until the free space was gone. Now, many of these animals have adopted our property. We have an abundance of gophers, birds of all varieties (including a team of roadrunners), a rabbit family and pack rat family.

Our experiences with the pack rats began about seven years ago when a family of them decided to move into our garage. When a tool would be missing I expected that one of our children had put it in their favorite forget me place, in the middle of the lawn, buried in the dog run or some such place. They found nothing wrong with leaving tools around since they knew where they were and the morning sprinkler shower would keep them clean and ready for the day to come. Sometimes, though, the rust would freeze up their works and the children could be heard banging them on some hard surface to loosen up the works.

One morning, Marilyn came to me complaining that her Camry would not start. Since I keep all vehicles in pristine condition, this didn't make sense. Sure enough, though, when I went to start the car, the silence was very loud. I popped the hood and all of the ignition wiring had been eaten through. A rattrap and three hundred dollars fixed the Camry. What I didn't know was that there wasn't just one pack rat, but an entire family living in the garage.

Two weeks later, I took the Camry down to the Toyota dealer for some minor work. Later in the day, I received a call from the mechanic. He said, "Did you drive your Camry down here?" "Why yes," I replied. He said, "Something has eaten all of the insulation from the spark plug wires. We cannot figure out how this car runs, but it does." Three hundred dollars later, another wiring harness and a bit of a temper set me in good humor to go looking for pack rats. I then checked my jeep and not one wire was touched, nor has it ever been. Upon closer inspection, every orange drop cord in the garage had been eaten through. A few days prior to this, when Marilyn went to wet mop our Saltillo tile, all of the strands of the mop had been carefully trimmed at their base.

All of this damage really upset me, so I moved the vehicles out of the garage and then unloaded the rest of its contents out onto the driveway. I love to work with wood and so have a nice collection of woodworking tools. In one corner of the garage is my collection of wood boards. Behind the wood was an entire family of pack rats. Now these are not New York rats, or ship rats, but they look like a king-size hamster with a long tail. They are cute, at the very least. In their nest were articles that had disappeared over the last year. All kinds of small tools, children's toys, toy figures from all around the neighborhood, shredded paper, wiring and a variety of collectibles that would make most children outrageously happy. In the midst of the nest were many of my missing tools that I had blamed the kids for losing. As soon as the nest was exposed the rats took off into parts unknown. Although some I helped to move into the next world forever, most made it into the yard and seemed to have disappeared.

Marilyn usually has simple "honey do" requests for me like, "Rick, would you get rid of the cactus in our yard?" type requests. This is no easy task considering the fact that ninety percent of the flora on our property is cactus and would fill half the city dump. It took several weeks and a trip to the eye surgeon (another story) but finally the deed was done. Only one problem, once again, I had done in the place of residence for the pack rat family. They responded by moving into our attic. It has been a very uneasy relationship for both of us. No matter how many traps I set, they were craftier. They became particularly active just as we were lying down to sleep. We could hear them racing back and forth between the ceiling and the insulation. I could imagine tons of rat stuff being deposited from one end of the attic to the other. Each night the visions of rat manure turning into mountains and flowing out of the vents in our roof would crowd out my rest as the rats would begin their nightly escapades.


Another one of these minor projects that my lovely wife contrived for me was to replace some of the warping wood up under the eaves or outside overhand of the roof. One early afternoon I was dutifully replacing sheets of plywood under the overhang of our roof. The overhang is about three and a half feet--no small project to pull down and replace. It is all work up over your head. I first removed the trim molding so that I could replace it after the new pieces of plywood were installed. Next, I pulled about half of the nails so that the first sheet of plywood would come down without damaging those around it. I removed most of the nails on the down slope side and then reached up and gave a mighty pull. The edge of the plywood came loose. As most men understand, when working over our heads and pulling on things, we always work with our mouths open. I don't quite understand it, but maybe it is like a woman who makes all kinds of funny faces and lip movements while spoon feeding her infant children. Anyway, I stabilized myself on the ladder, and gave the plywood sheet a yank, having carefully placed one hand on each side of the sheet. Down came one end of the plywood and with it about a ton of rat poop.

Before that moment, I had never tasted rat poop, nor had I ever in my life taken a rat poop shower. It not only filled my open mouth, but also went down my shirt, and every other place that needed filling. Even the tops of my loose fitting socks became receptacles for this unheavenly mixture. I am somewhat bald, with reddish grey hair. Since I am a red head, my skin is usually very fair. I jumped off of the ladder and fell to the ground while the rest of the infernal flow continued to cover my back. When I came to my senses, the flow had stopped, but I was now dark brown from head to foot. In Tucson, it sometimes gets hot. On this particular day it was about 116 in the shade. Needless to say, I was covered in sweat. Dry rat poop and sweat make an interesting mixture. One seems to stick rather well to the other. I think that I must have spit the stuff out of my mouth and blew it out of my nose for days. You cannot imagine the flavor that it gives to food once it has tainted your sinuses.

I walked over to the front porch and rang the doorbell. I was greeted with peals of laughter from my lovely wife who slammed the door. There I was, stranded on the front porch in my newly acquired attire.

This was only the beginning of our attempts to get rats out of our attic and to repair their ongoing damage. When we replaced the roof and had the entire fascia board repaired or replaced, the persistent critters ate a three-inch hole through the two-inch facial board. Every time I would plug it up, they would re-eat their way through. Finally, the events of a fine spring day settled the matter once and for all. A very large swarm of killer bees decided to take residence in our attic. They, of course, found easy access through the three-inch hole. As they took over the attic, they drove the pack rats out. Now we only had "killer bees!" The hole was almost over the front door to our home. Matters started getting a bit worse when they started coming into the house through a variety of small openings in vents and recessed light fixtures.

By this time we were almost ready to welcome the rats back, but not quite yet. I called our insurance company, and they said, "Get a bee keeper! Oh! By the way, do you still have rats in your attic?" I was thinking, "Why? Do they want to cancel my policy?" "No" I said. "We just have killer bees." The beekeeper arrived the next day, killed the bees that chased off the rats never to be seen or heard from again and I re-plugged the hole with cement.

We breathed a sigh of relief several days later after the hive decided not to take up residence again on our property.

Some Days are Better Than Others!

# Chapter 5

# A Boy and His Dog

When I was a boy, dogs were my constant companions. Marilyn had cats when she was growing up. I had to introduce her to dogs, just as she introduced me to cats.

One day my parents told me about a dog that worked on a ranch herding cattle, but had found a taste for fresh chicken. Besides herding, she was also a great jumper. I don't mean that she jumped hurdles for a living like some horses. Pookie jumped fences up to eight feet high just for fun. She had a good nature as well. A smile always graced her countenance. It looked more like she was laughing at her human companions.

Once she found a taste for fowl, her ranching days ended. The rancher and his family loved her, but unless she found a non-farm family, her life would be over. I am not sure how we heard about her desperate straits, but one day my parents and I ended up on a large spread in Napa valley. We wanted to find out if she would accept us.

I will never forget that day. We drove up this beautiful tree lined road to an area by the barn. I spotted a medium sized, black curly dog. She lay chained to a center stake within an eight-foot high enclosure. When we laid eyes on one another, it was mutually love at first sight. She was never much of a barker unless we were teasing each other. She stood, smiled as if to say, "It is about time you got here!" I asked the rancher, "Why is she chained inside such a tall fence?" He replied, "I haven't seen a fence, yet, that she can't jump."

The rancher sized up all of my five-foot height and said, "Are you man enough for that dog?" Usually, I am one to analyze someone before I answer. This time was no different. I stood there staring at him. My first thought was, "Man enough? I am here, aren't I?" I am from a military family; youngsters are not smart mouthed with adults. The reply is usually expected to be, "Yes, sir." or, "No sir." (Or some other short answer with sir or mam attached to the end.) I decided not to answer his question, but instead I asked him a question. "Sir, can I take her home with me?" There was a strange glint in his eyes. It was obvious that he made a great effort not to break out laughing. He answered, "Well, you look man enough, so go get her."

What I didn't know was that my parents had already been there to find out about Pookie. I guess she passed the test.

The rancher and my parents didn't seem like strangers to one another either. Mom and dad are very well read and it was no surprise to me that my dog came with a very distinctive name from one of Rudyard Kipling's books. I never did think that the rancher called her Pook, but that was the name that she was introduced with. Somehow, I think that her first owner would have called her something like "Bet" or "Dog." I just adjusted and called her Pookie, which she seemed to prefer.

Pookie was intelligent but I think that she could also read minds. She knew thoughts like "ride," "walk," "fish" or "camping." Except when she was desperate, and wanted out, she always was eager to learn something new. She was always intuitively aware of my needs and moods.

Challenges like "speak" and "shake hands" were for everyday run of the mill dogs. While she knew stuff like that, Pook knew hand signals. She could jump hurdles, or go through the most difficult contest challenges by following them. Frequently, though, she would just ignore the hand signals and complete her tasks without any help.

Everyone always complimented me on how well I had trained her, but she was really the one that trained people.

All through grade school and the first two years of high school we were inseparable. Finally, though, as a junior in high school, I went away to a military school. Up to this point my twin had been a straight A student and no matter how hard I worked I struggled to get anything above a D or F. I thought that if I could just go to a military school and learn better self-discipline that I could excel.

After taking my pre-admission testing the dean called my parents in for a chat, "Your son is highly intelligent and disciplined but he is facing some challenges in his life. He is dyslexic and reads at less than a third grade level. Before he can enter our school, he must learn how to read." He then supplied a list of specialists. They were so good that in just four months my reading level advanced to a junior in College. That is probably why concepts like "can't" and "it is impossible" are so foreign to me. It was a time when wonderful teachers opened up vast new worlds for me. However, they never got me to stop being creative when it comes to spelling and punctuation.

I adapted to school easily but Pookie couldn't adjust to being without her master. She had to befriend my twin sister, a girl. Now I must say, there is nothing wrong with girls, Pook was one, but she was a man's dog. She didn't enjoy wearing bonnets and dresses. She was a dog of the rugged outdoors, and she just wasn't into girl's activities.

When I would come home on some weekends, we occasionally would go fishing together. Our favorite time was during the striped bass runs up the Sacramento River and its tributaries. Most weekend fishermen don't know this, but big bass follow reed lines along the banks of the river (especially during high tide.) All of the nutrients are there so the smaller fish of other species come there to feed. The big bass eat this plentiful bounty. The younger bass love the center of the river and they rush mad long, not unlike a bunch of teenagers going somewhere because everyone else is. Weekenders unfailingly rent boats and head for the middle of the river. There they sit, catching small bass as fast as they can bait their hooks.

My grandfather was an excellent fisherman who taught me how to search out all kinds of edible salt and freshwater species. Rather than rent a boat, we would find a pleasant tributary spot and then figure how best to get there. Usually it meant getting a rancher's permission to walk across his land. Most of them were very cordial to a boy and his dog. Since we were fishing, we would be no danger to their expensive cattle. They always made us promise to come by their house to show what we had caught. Since we usually caught our limit, we would leave several good-sized fish as a thank you. A little kindness returned was always remembered during the next season.

On this particular occasion, Pook and I went to visit a rancher that we knew as Mr. Jake. He was glad to see us and as usual wanted to see if our bait or tackle had changed from the year before. In the years before, Mr. Jake raised some cattle, but mostly alfalfa and wheat. His ranch went on as far as you could possibly see. Most ranchers are understated. This is not to say that they lack any intelligence. They have huge responsibilities and not many people to share them with. When they speak, it is usually frank and to the point. This time Mr. Jake said, "Rick, you and Pook might keep an extra eye out for some of my new cattle." There was a lot in what he didn't say. "Yes sir!" We replied. We had to walk through a number of fields, several miles, until we reached our favorite spot. The tributary had dug away at the bank until it was fairly steep, forming a ten foot ledge. Below this ledge the water eddied and here was where big fish came to feed.

Pook would lie down next to me in the grass and listen to me as I talked to the fish, nature and her. When she would get bored with the conversation she would go off on a run for a while. We had already caught two 20 lb. bass and I was working on preparing my rig for a larger one.

Pook was a wonderful dog. She was always finding ways to gain my approval. She would bring me a variety of things when we were on these trips together. Pieces of drift wood, unusual stones, and sometimes she would herd the occasional jack rabbit my way, just to show that she hadn't lost her touch. Then, with a big smile on her face, she would come and lay down by me once again.

This time I used larger hooks and a whole mackerel. On my first cast, the line began to travel against the stream of the river. A large fish had picked it up. I lifted the pole tip and off we were. This was a monster. I let him run for a while and then he settled down to a good strong pull. I must say my full attention was on the fish. I started working him down the bank where the drop wasn't so steep. About 50 feet down stream it was only about a four foot drop to the muddy water and shore.

The ground shook; it isn't too unusual to have quaking ground in California. I was surrounded by rolling, grassy hills and could see no reason for the tremors so I just kept fighting the fish. It just couldn't get any better!

Then, in the distance, I heard Pook barking. It was a happy "having fun" kind of bark. The tremors increased. Still no sign of Pook but her barking kept increasing in volume as did the intensity of the tremor. By now, sound accompanied the tremors. My attention was constantly divided between the fish, my dog and the alarming circumstances. About one hundred and fifty feet away was a rolling hilltop which seemed to be the direction of all of the excitement. One second it was a wonderful pastoral scene and next, one of absolute terror. Pookie was bringing me a herd of about one hundred and fifty head of Brahma breeding cattle complete with one very unhappy bull. Pook was not in sight. She was far behind the herd. When she did clear the ridge there was so much noise she couldn't hear me over the cattle and I wasn't about to turn loose of my prized fish to give her hand signals. My thoughts and emotions went through a variety of instant moods and colors from joy to concern until Pook turned the heard at me. Here they came at full gait. Everything turned to pure terror when the Brahma bull spotted me, lowered his head and came raging forward like a red-eyed steam locomotive. It wasn't hard to read his mind. He wanted to kill something and I was it!

All this time I had been running down the bank, still trying to reel in my fish. The herd was now about fifty feet away. The bull was about fifteen feet in front of the herd. He had one thing in mind- my hide and it had a big red mark on it where he intended to run me through.

I got to the place where the bank was about four feet above the water and I took a flying leap right into the river. Not for a moment did I ever consider letting go of the fish. I have always been a very strong swimmer and was dressed in light-weight clothes and shoes. Just as I hit the water, Pook raced to the head of the herd, barked a few times and off they all went into another direction. As she passed by, she gave me a big smile as if to say, "See, I haven't forgotten how!"

She laughed as if to ask, "What are you doing?"

Somehow I worked myself down the bank without losing my rod, reel and fish or my life. I finally got to a place along the bank where I could get out. There I was, covered with river "yuk" from head to foot-but I still had my fish. Following a few more minutes fight, it was finally landed. Certainly the biggest striped bass I had ever caught. As I look back through the passing imagination of my mind, it must have weighed at least 100 lbs.-but actually it was closer to thirty or so.

Pook happily returned. Her gait was filled with all of the music that happiness and fulfillment reflect. There we were, a once again proven, content, cattle dog and a happy but clay brown boy. It was a time of true contentment and happiness-the kind that only a boy and his dog can happily experience. We collected the tackle box and the two other fish and sloshed off towards the ranch house.

Mr. and Mrs. Jake were sitting under one of their huge patio shade trees. As soon as we came into sight they began to point and laugh. Mr. Jake actually fell out of his chair he was laughing so hard. Behind a very dirty boy with tackle and three very large fish, and a prancing dog, all one hundred and fifty head of his new herd, less the bull, quietly followed. They must have all thought that Pook was their mother. With a hand wave, Pook took the Brahmas off somewhere and then returned alone.

Mrs. Jake had baked cookies and set out lemonade for us all. Pook was rewarded with a big piece of raw meat and water. Her look said, "Could life ever be better?" I handed Mr. and Mrs. Jake my prized catch and one of the other fish. I knew that they would have a freezer big enough for them and my mom would appreciate it more if we left room in our military refrigerator for other kinds of food as well.

Mr. Jake never said a word to me about how muddy I was, but he kept looking at Pook, giving her a big wink and then he would just laugh. You know, I have often wondered if Pook hadn't worked for that rancher sometime in her past. When we got home, my mom asked, "How in the world did you get so dirty?" Moms should know better when it comes to sons. I replied, "I lost my balance and fell into the river!" Seeing me standing there, I guess she knew it was too late to worry. Events like this were not infrequent.

Pook has long since gone, but I can't help but remember some of the wonderful things that I learned from that dog. No matter how big the obstacle, there is always a way to deal with it. Moreover, no matter how old you may be, you never lose your true value and abilities to the One who created you.

Pook always faced every new challenge with a smile and a happy spirit. I wasn't with her when she died. I understand that her last moments passed while dreaming. I have often thought that dream place could have been of the time when she joyously showed her young redheaded master how much she loved him. After all, that herd was a gift that she knew how to deliver. I think that today she fills heaven's space with barks of laughter and joy and certainly she fills the lives of other children who are there.

# Chapter 6
# Camping Trip from Hell

I must say, none of our vacations have been boring. Just before flying to China to adopt LanJu, Marilyn and I purchased a Coleman Camping Trailer and we headed for the White Mountains in northern Arizona. We ended up in a beautiful Federal Campground near a little village called Greer. There is something special that happens to the human spirit as gentle wind passes through lush pine trees. We hadn't camped in a number of years. Ah! This was the life! It was a final rest before spending two eventful weeks in China.

Seven months later, prior to going on a thirteen state trip with Lexi, we decided that we would test drive our older Jeep Cherokee and its ability to pull our trailer. We struck off for Prescott, Arizona. Since we hadn't made reservations, we ended up in a RV park overlooking a half dried up lake. We knew that we were in trouble by the many rows of bug repellent cans in the camping store. Little did we know that the half-dried up lake was a breeding ground for mosquitoes of all shapes and sizes, their intent was the same, to painfully dip into our individual blood supply.

The sunset was beautiful as we relaxed outside playing table games with Lexi. All of a sudden we were chased into our trailer by vicious winged creatures with oversized appetites for our blood. Once inside we discovered that camping trailers have all kinds of little holes that mosquitoes can wiggle their way through on their determined journey to feed on us. I got a roll of toilet paper and began to plug all of the crevices where these dastardly biting insects were gaining entry. It seemed the more holes I plugged and the darker it got outside, the more places they found to get in. We all ran for our beds and turned the lights out while listening to the tormenting sound of mosquitoes. Eventually we all went to sleep. At first light we noticed that all of the blood thirsty creatures had somehow exited the same way they arrived.

We all breathed a sigh of relief and I proceeded to get the grills on the trailer ready for breakfast only to find that someone had tampered with the gas regulator. We were not only camped next to a stinking lake fill with mosquitoes, but we couldn't cook food either. I finally sorted out the problem with the regulator and fixed it by late morning. We spent the rest of the day just having fun enjoying Prescott.

Gusty winds kept the mosquitoes at bay, and we had a great evening. When the sun came up the next morning, it seemed like a great beginning to a wonderful day. It was time to return to Tucson. I am an early riser so I went and put gas in the Jeep. I did notice a slight gasoline smell, but there was a gas spill in the next lane at the gas station.

We took our time packing up the trailer, and then I hooked it up to the Jeep and called for Lexi and Marilyn to pile in. Marilyn said, "I smell gas!" I responded, "You probably do, I just filled the tank." I carefully pulled out of the horrible campground and we all cheered as we left. Deciding to return to Prescott to pick up a few things for our trip, we took a mountainous route into town.

Just as we cleared the forest and the business section began to appear, Marilyn shouted, "Rick, I smell gas!" One of my problems is that I cannot smell. So I responded, "Honey I don't smell anything." Marilyn then shouted with increased excitement, "I don't smell gas anymore I smell smoke." I was in the middle of saying to her that I didn't smell any smoke when I noticed the paint on the hood burning off from the inside out. I quickly turned up the next street. We just cleared the main highway when the engine quit. All of the wires had burned through. We all bailed out of the car like rats in a sinking ship. People came running out of businesses yelling pop the hood and I'll put the fire out. I shouted back, "I am not putting my hands in there, let it burn." By that time the fire department arrived, and they efficiently put out the fire." The fireman said, "It is a good thing that you didn't open that hood some people have tried and lost their hands or eyes."

Our car was towed to Jeep and there we sat in the waiting room for a prognosis. The repair staff was limited on Saturday, so it took all afternoon before we got the final word, "Your car is totaled." We cleaned out all of our personal possessions and a kind salesman took us to our trailer.

Friends of ours had towed the trailer to the only campground that had an opening. We ended up right back in the campground from hell.

We look back on the experience now and laugh, but then we thought, "Some days are just better than others."

# Chapter 7

## DEAD OR ALIVE IT'S OFF TO SCHOOL

Actually, I begin praying for calmness months before school starts. I drive an aging Toyota Camry and normal cars look big in the rear view mirror. I have only just now recovered from last school year. Tucson is filled with thousands of huge S.U.V.'s driven by mothers who are trying to juggle the schedules of all of their children and still make it to work on time.

I am amazed at all of the things that late mothers can do while rushing madly towards their destinations. Just before school got out this last year, I was going the speed limit in my neighborhood and a huge black Chevrolet Suburban turned on to the road behind me, within seconds it was pasted on my car's rear bumper. When the oncoming traffic flow stopped, the mom passed over the double line, went through the intersection on the wrong side of the street and sped rapidly out of sight. That was amazing enough, but she was yelling at the kids in her vehicle, combing her hair, eating a cup of yogurt and all the while talking on her cell phone.

I am always shocked that I actually survived the driving antics of mom's rushing here and there. Just the thought of having to pull out of my calm "country" neighborhood early in the morning and face mom's and their kid's taxi's often turns my stomach.

I cannot for the life of me figure out why I survive from school year to school year with all of the mom taxi drivers. I know most men feel the same. Our blood runs cold when the grill of an S.U.V. fills the rear view mirror and a frantic, multi-tasking mom is behind the wheel.

You know, guys are predictable. When they drive up on your rear bumper, they just think that they are in the Indy 500. They are simply going to compete for the space that your car occupies. If you are on the freeway and they are creeping along, when you go to pass them they accelerate so that you can't pass. With moms, you just never know what they will do.

We live in Vail, Arizona. I am not sure what the population is because it increases by what seems like several thousand people every day. Vail, is known for its very active railroad tracks. One set goes west and the other goes east. These tracks are only about 100 yards apart. It is almost always the case, that when in a hurry, trains two miles long are sailing across the highway with horns blowing and red lights flashing.

On the South and North sides of these tracks are two high schools, a middle school and an elementary school that is full. Every day that I come into town I face moms behind me and in front of me. It is one of the most frightful things a man can face.

Just before the school year ended for the summer I decided to play it safe and go in the Expedition to the kid's school. We have three children and each went to a different school. We had five minutes before the middle school bell would ring and we were just loading into the truck. As we turned onto the road I thought, "This is the life," "Safe at last!"

About a mile from the first drop point, I turned to talk with Marilyn. She was digging around in her purse, putting lipstick on and direction the children while she drove. Ah! I would rather be in a Mom's Taxi than in front of it.

# Chapter 8

## Men Definitely are Not Women

When praying the other morning I began to think about all of the things that Marilyn does for our family. How little did I know that later in that day that I would come face to face with motherhood myself.

My thoughts turned to the Biblical book of Titus, and I wondered about the roles of women.

Titus 2:3-5 (NIV)

*Likewise, teach the older women to be reverent in the way they live, not to be slanderers or addicted to much wine, but to teach what is good. [4] Then they can train the younger women to love their husbands and children, [5] to be self-controlled and pure, to be busy at home, to be kind, and to be subject to their husbands, so that no one will malign the word of God.*

As a guy, I don't always appreciate everything that my wife does. She usually looks unruffled, hair combed, makeup in place, the kids started with their homework and dinner under way when I walk in the door around dinner time. I recently had foot surgery, and was forced to be at home with my leg elevated to prevent blood clots and other side-affects. A week after surgery while using crutches and rather tired of sitting in one place, I said to Marilyn, "Go ahead and go to your bible study I'll watch the kids. It is normally our practice for me to watch our three young children and Marilyn attends one of our small group meetings. Since it was our oldest daughter's clarinet lesson day, she took our very together and helpful Lexi with her. I was left alone with our three and seven year olds.

Marilyn had done the wash but didn't have time to put it away and a few dishes needing to be washed. Sarah had homework to do and Liana was given tasks to do because she loves to help. Even though I was trapped at home, I had my laptop and the phone to do all kinds of pastoral duties. I was in the middle of a call when Marilyn waved goodbye. That was when everything began to fall apart. Marilyn prepared a nice crock-pot meal. I carefully dished out dinner to my two youngest. The three year old gobbled her dinner down and began to shout, "I am the winner!" Sarah, not to be out done consumed everything except the cooked carrots and onions. Those she quickly discarded into our small dog's bowl. I helped Sarah write a story about Cinderella and then sent her out to the dining room table to copy her story on her assignment paper.

Liana and I began running more wash, sorting it to prepare putting it away. The two of us sorted all of the clothes and then put them away. Sarah and Liana and I made our king size bed. Not too bad for someone on crutches.

I felt like everything was under control. I called Marilyn just before the small group started and told her how organized everything was and that the wash had been finished and put away. When I mentioned that we made the bed. Marilyn said, "I knew I shouldn't have left home. You are supposed to be sitting with your leg up!" I didn't mention that I wasn't using the crutches either.

Sarah was back to her homework, Liana was off organizing and I was working once again on a future sermon. All of a sudden, Sarah starts yelling, "Daddy the cats ruined my paper!" One of our more curious cats knocked over a cup of water onto Sarah's paper and then ran across the wet paper tearing her school work. I took the soggy paper and dried it with Marilyn's hairdryer. My daughter said, "Maybe the teacher won't notice the holes." The dog began eating the uneaten vegetables, and then raced off to the freshly cleaned bedroom. She jumped up on the bed and threw up all over the bed. It was so juicy that it soaked through the designer bed spread, freshly washed blankets and sheets. My three year old had been up on the bed "cleaning it up" when I arrived on the scene. She in fact was sitting in the middle of the mess grinding it into the bed getting it all over her as well. Sarah started shouting, "Daddy, I am going to throw up." Funny, I was thinking the same thing. That happened within the first hour of Marilyn leaving, and I wondered, "Will we survive another three hours before Marilyn gets home?" I thought, "Boy men really are different than women!"

# Chapter 9

## "When He Loves Me Does He Really Love Me?"

Col. 3:19 (NIV)

*Husbands, love your wives and do not be harsh with them.*

I often think of the various ways that I attempt to fulfill these words.

I usually get up before the stars fade and the sun's radiance opens the darkened sky of dawn. On this particular morning I was visiting the place of twilight dreams when my thoughts projected themselves to the first words that I would express when my wife would waken. I felt a warm caress across the top of my balding head. Still mostly asleep, I opened my eyes and looked into two deep, dark pools of love. I thought to myself, "Could life be any better?"

My wife doesn't need to talk to express her love for me. What words could I say to reveal my love in a way that would sink deep into her heart? I reached out to touch her head. It was then that a long tongue penetrated my nose. Yow! This wasn't Marilyn it was her miniature, doctor "Seussian" dog. Isn't it interesting how many things intrude into our relationships between us and our wives?

One of the ways that I express my love for Marilyn is to father our girls. Sometimes, though, I get a glance into my wife's world.

Every now and then, I get a glimpse of what it must be like to be a mother. My thoughts returned to one event that seemed like an eternity. I went into the master bathroom to brush my teeth following breakfast. Marilyn was in the shower, Lexi, Sarah and Liana our three Chinese adopted daughters, all followed me there. If you know Sarah, you know that she is a non-stop communicator. She began talking to me as I was attempting to direct my thoughts towards the day. Lexi, also, began talking to both Sarah and I. Lexi was giving directions to Sarah more than anything else, and Liana was saying something as well. Curiously, Liana kept lifting the toilet lid, looking into the toilet, and then looking at me. She would then close the lid look at me and start the cycle all over again. In the midst of the clamor, I was still brushing my teeth until I realized that

Liana was attempting to tell me that she had to go to the bathroom. While still brushing my teeth, I took Liana's sleeper off and pulled down on her pull ups only to have two large, dark logs fall onto the floor. I got down on my hands and knees to clean up the mess. Sarah stooped down so that her mouth was next to my ear so that she could continue her one way conversation. I held Liana with one hand and attempted to sanitize the floor with the other. Lexi continued to give Sarah directions. Now, very distracted, I pulled too hard on Liana's pull ups and she fell down - into the toilet. Now, I have a bottom- wet - baby who is crying. Sarah is still talking and Lexi is still giving directions. I am generally fairly cool and collected, but now find that I have broken out into a cold sweat. I feel the tension building. My world view has shrunk to the size of the bathroom, and I am thinking . . . "Let me out of here!"

Every now and then, I get a glimpse of what it must be like to be a mother. The event that I just described only lasted about thirty seconds in real time, but in father time must have been at least ten hours. I, then, decided I needed to be at work. I left the somewhat wet baby, talking Sarah and directing Lexi in

Marilyn's motherly care. I wondered if she were asking the question, "When he says he loves me does he really love me?"

Made in the USA
San Bernardino, CA
13 July 2018